P9-DDW-752

10 LEADERS
WHO CHANGED THE WORLD

Written by Clive Gifford
Illustrated by David Cousens

KINGFISHER
NEW YORK

Additional illustrations by Sarah Cousens

Copyright © 2008 by Macmillan Children's Books
KINGFISHER
Published in The United States by Kingfisher, an imprint of Henry Holt
and Company LLC, 175 Fifth Avenue, New York, New York 10010. First
published in Great Britain by Kingfisher Publications plc, an imprint of
Macmillan Children's Books, London.
All rights reserved

Distributed in Canada by H. B. Fenn and Company Ltd.

Library of Congress Cataloging-in-Publication Data
has been applied for.

ISBN: 978-0-7534-6104-4

Kingfisher books are available for special promotions and premiums.
For details contact: Director of Special Markets, Holtzbrinck Publishers.

First American Edition October 2008
Printed in Singapore
10 9 8 7 6 5 4 3 2 1
1TR/0608/TWP/MAR/150MA/C

Mohandas Gandhi

Mao Zedong

Franklin Delano
Roosevelt

Contents

Winston Churchill

Mohandas Gandhi

April 6, 1930. A small 60-year-old man dressed in a traditional dhoti loincloth bent down by the sea in Dandi, India, and scooped up a handful of salt. Three weeks earlier he had set out with 78 other people on a 235-mi. (380-km) walk from Sabarmati. Now, his simple act was watched by thousands of people. In a country ruled—sometimes brutally—by the British, Mohandas Gandhi had just broken the law. No Indian was allowed to collect his or her own salt. Gandhi encouraged others to do the same, and within months more than 50,000 people had been arrested by the British forces, himself included. He would continue to protest peacefully until his beloved India won independence.

Gandhi was born in Porbandar, on the western coast of India. His father became the *diwan* (prime minister) of nearby Rajkot when he was seven years old, and as a young boy, Gandhi grew up in comfortable surroundings.

Gandhi's protest was against the British salt tax, which made it illegal for Indians to collect salt from seashores and lakeshores. Instead, they were forced to buy it at high prices that they could not afford.

Gandhi married Kasturba Makanji in an arranged ceremony when they were both 13 years old.

Gandhi's mother was a devout Hindu who often fasted (didn't eat any food) as part of her religion. He was a small, shy child and an average student with sloppy handwriting. When Gandhi was 16, his father died. Against his mother's wishes, he took a seven-week trip by sea to train as a lawyer in London, England. His wife and young son stayed in India.

Gandhi tried hard to fit in with British customs of the time. He took violin, dance, French, and speech lessons and wore fashionable clothes. But he was desperately homesick and lonely. Eventually, he met like-minded people at the London Vegetarian Society and among the theosophists, a group who tried to find links between all the world's religions. He read both the Bible and the epic Hindu poem the *Bhagavad Gita* for the first time.

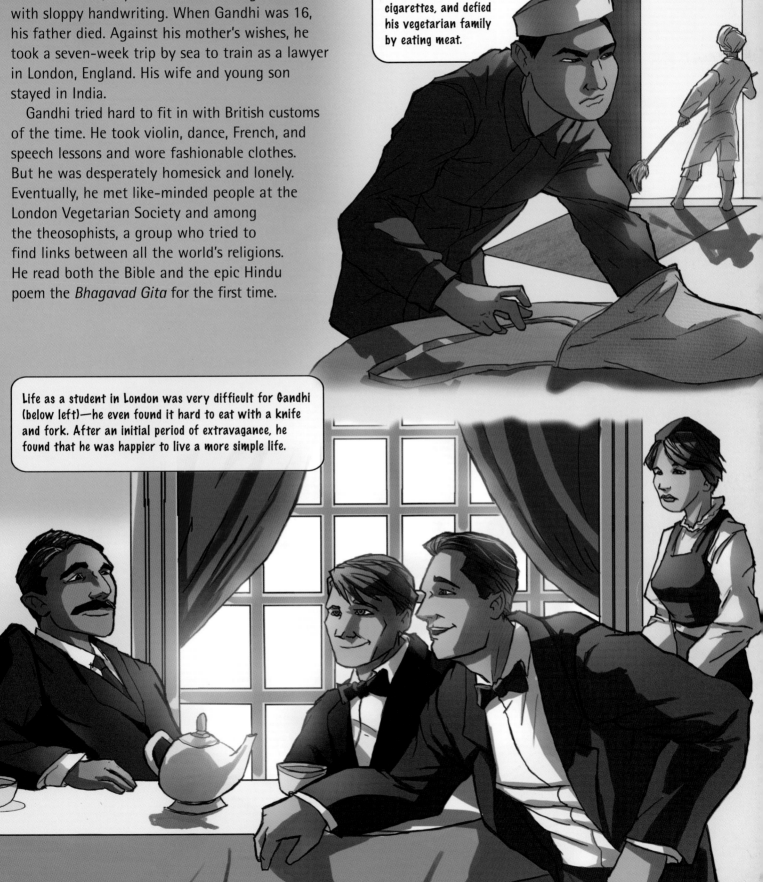

Gandhi went through a period of teenage rebellion. He stole from servants, smoked cigarettes, and defied his vegetarian family by eating meat.

Life as a student in London was very difficult for Gandhi (below left)—he even found it hard to eat with a knife and fork. After an initial period of extravagance, he found that he was happier to live a more simple life.

After finishing law school, Gandhi returned to India in 1891, but for two years only. His mother had died while he was away, and he found it difficult to find work. He took a legal job with an Indian company in South Africa. Up until this time, Gandhi had led a fairly privileged life as a member of the Indian middle class. In South Africa, he was shocked by the way the country's 65,000 Indian immigrants were treated as second-class citizens. He planned to live there for one year, but he stayed for 20.

Gandhi's time in South Africa was eventful. His family joined him in 1897. He set up his own legal practice in Johannesburg, formed an ambulance corps of around 1,100 volunteers to help save lives during the Boer War, founded a news journal called *Indian Opinion*, and set up an ashram (spiritual community).

On a train to Pretoria in 1893, Gandhi was thrown out of a first-class train car simply because he was not white.

He spent the night, shivering in the cold at Pietermaritzburg railroad station.

Later, he was beaten up by a stagecoach driver who refused to let him sit inside. Gandhi was shocked into taking action—he lost his shyness and began to fight for the rights of Indians.

Gandhi developed a way to protest without violence, naming it Satyagraha—"truth and determination" in the Sanskrit language. He was attacked and imprisoned, which only developed his calm determination. Thousands of Indians joined him, standing up for their rights by marching peacefully or refusing to obey unfair laws. In 1914, the South African government gave in to some of their demands.

Gandhi founded Tolstoy farm in 1910. There, Indians worked together to be self-sufficient, and Gandhi lived the simplest life possible.

Gandhi returned to India in 1915. Except for a trip to London in 1931, he never left his home country again. He became the leader of the INC (Indian National Congress) party after World War I and traveled throughout the nation, urging Indians to join him in campaigns of noncooperation against British rule.

Thousands joined Gandhi's noncooperation campaign, burning and boycotting British goods and leaving British schools and jobs.

The 1919 Rowlett Act gave Great Britain emergency powers in India. A protest against them in the holy Sikh city of Amritsar turned into a bloodbath, with British troops killing or wounding more than 1,500 people.

Thousands of Indians were arrested. In 1922, Gandhi himself was sentenced to six years in prison. He was set free after two years and appeared to leave politics, but he was busy trying to improve relations between Hindus and Muslims in India. Many thought of him as a saint and started to call him *Mahatma*, which means "great spirit" in Sanskrit.

Gandhi returned to London in 1931 for three months of talks about India's future. Four years later, the British allowed Indians to take some control in governing their country.

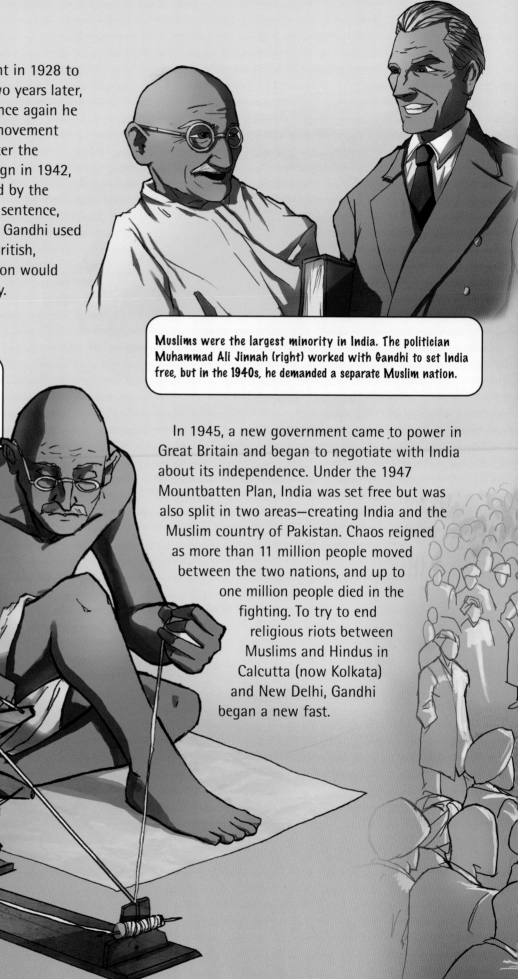

Gandhi returned to the spotlight in 1928 to organize a strike against taxes. Two years later, he led the salt march to Dandi. Once again he became the driving force of the movement to free India from British rule. After the launch of the "Quit India" campaign in 1942, many INC leaders were imprisoned by the British. During Gandhi's two-year sentence, his wife, Kasturba, died. In prison, Gandhi used fasting as a weapon against the British, who feared that a bloody revolution would follow if he were to die in custody.

Muslims were the largest minority in India. The politician Muhammad Ali Jinnah (right) worked with Gandhi to set India free, but in the 1940s, he demanded a separate Muslim nation.

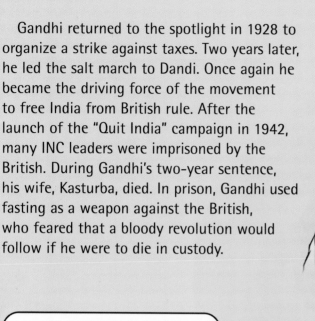

Many Indians could buy only British clothes, so Gandhi taught himself to make cotton cloth, spinning threads on a simple wheel. He encouraged all Indians to do the same.

In 1945, a new government came to power in Great Britain and began to negotiate with India about its independence. Under the 1947 Mountbatten Plan, India was set free but was also split in two areas—creating India and the Muslim country of Pakistan. Chaos reigned as more than 11 million people moved between the two nations, and up to one million people died in the fighting. To try to end religious riots between Muslims and Hindus in Calcutta (now Kolkata) and New Delhi, Gandhi began a new fast.

In January 1948, 12 days after the end of another, final fast, a frail Gandhi went to pray at Birla House in New Delhi, accompanied by his grandnieces Manu and Abha. Around 500 people were there to meet him, including Nathuram Godse, a Hindu extremist who believed that Gandhi had been too sympathetic to Muslims. At point-blank range, Godse fired three bullets into Gandhi's body. The Mahatma fell to the ground, unconscious. Moments later, he was dead.

Gandhi's teachings and life have been an inspiration to many campaigners, from Nelson Mandela in South Africa to the American civil rights leader Martin Luther King, Jr. Gandhi himself contended that he was nowhere close to being a saint; he was just an ordinary man who had actually failed to reach many of his goals. But today millions revere him as a saintly figure and the father of modern India.

Nathuram Godse shot Gandhi because he thought that the Mahatma had betrayed Hindus. A bomb had gone off at Birla House days before, but Gandhi refused extra security.

More than one million people mourned at Mohandas Gandhi's funeral. The pyre burned for 14 hours, and his ashes were divided and scattered on India's major rivers.

LIFE LINK
One of Gandhi's most outspoken opponents was Winston Churchill, who wanted to keep India under British rule. During World War II, when Gandhi was on a hunger strike in prison, British ministers had to persuade Churchill to release Gandhi and not let him starve to death.

Winston Churchill

December 1899. Winston Churchill lay at the bottom of a deep mineshaft and hoped that the rats would stay away. Days earlier, he had leaped over a prison camp fence, walked along a railroad track, jumped aboard a moving train, and hidden under a pile of filthy coal sacks to avoid being captured. By chance he had met a British engineer, who lowered him into the mine in order to escape the Boer soldiers who were scouring the land above for him.

It had been a momentous year for the 25-year-old. Before sailing to South Africa to work as a journalist in the Boer War, he had resigned from the British army and had tried but failed to become a member of parliament (MP) in northwest England.

After his capture by the Boers, he wasted little time in escaping, without the aid of either a map or a compass. On December 21, safe on the African coast, he wired the story of his escape—a perilous trek of more than 250 mi. (400km)—back home to Great Britain.

The Boers were Dutch settlers fighting against British rule. On November 15, 1899, they ambushed a British army train. Churchill (far right) rescued several injured soldiers and tried to get the train moving again, but he was captured and taken to a prison camp.

As a boy, Churchill spent hours creating battle formations with his toy soldiers. His father was a politician, and his mother was the daughter of an American millionaire. Both parents were too busy to spend much time with their young son.

Churchill was born into a wealthy family, but he was a rebellious schoolboy. He passed his military school exams on the third attempt, but his low grade meant that he could not join the infantry. He trained as a cavalryman and started playing polo with such enthusiasm that he even begged his mother for the money to buy a stable of polo ponies.

Churchill was an enthusiastic polo player. His last game was in 1927, at the age of 52.

Between 1895 and 1898, he participated in three military campaigns, each one on a different continent. He traveled to Cuba with Spanish forces and was also stationed in India and the Sudan. To earn extra money, he worked as a war reporter during all three postings. In 1899 he had his first novel, *Savriola*, published.

In 1898 Churchill participated in one of the last-ever British cavalry charges, in the battle of Omdurman in the Sudan.

Back in Great Britain after his escape from the Boers, Churchill won a seat as an MP (member of parliament) in 1900. It was the start of a political career that would last for 60 years. Six years later he entered the inner circle of the government as a cabinet minister, and in 1910 he became the home secretary. By the time World War I broke out, he was in charge of the Royal Navy.

Churchill was one of the first leaders to see that aircraft could be useful during a war. He helped form the Royal Naval Air Service in 1912 and even took flying lessons himself before World War I (above).

In 1915 more than 200,000 soldiers, many from Australia and New Zealand, died in the battles in Gallipoli, on the coast of Turkey. Churchill was demoted as a result.

Churchill's career took a battering after the disastrous Gallipoli campaign in 1915. He rejoined the army to serve in the trenches of northern France, until he was called back to the government in 1917. After sensationally switching from the Liberal Party to the Conservatives, he became the chancellor of the exchequer and was in charge of Great Britain's economy between 1924 and 1929.

In the 1930s Churchill was on the political scrapheap. He was still an MP, but his party was not in power and he was mocked for supporting Great Britain's rule of India and for warning of the dangers of Nazi Germany under Adolf Hitler. He criticized the British government for giving in to Germany's demands in order to avoid war—a policy known as appeasement.

After the German invasion of Poland, Great Britain declared war on September 3, 1939. In November, Churchill took charge of the Royal Navy. Six months later Neville Chamberlain resigned as the prime minister and Churchill was chosen to lead a wartime government made up of all the major political parties. He was 65 years old, and his country faced its darkest hour in hundreds of years.

Churchill gives one of his many morale-boosting speeches to the House of Commons. He wrote the scripts himself, often taking up to 30 hours to complete each one.

During the Battle of Britain in 1940, a British Spitfire fighter plane (right) shoots down a German Dornier bomber. Despite being outnumbered, British planes managed to repel the German air force.

As German forces stormed the continent, Great Britain became more and more isolated. Some politicians wanted to surrender, but Churchill was determined to stand firm. He asked the House of Commons to support his inner government circle, known as the War Cabinet, declaring, "I have nothing to offer but blood, toil, tears, and sweat." It was the first of many powerful speeches that lifted the spirits of the entire country.

Churchill holds up two fingers to give his famous wartime sign—"V for victory."

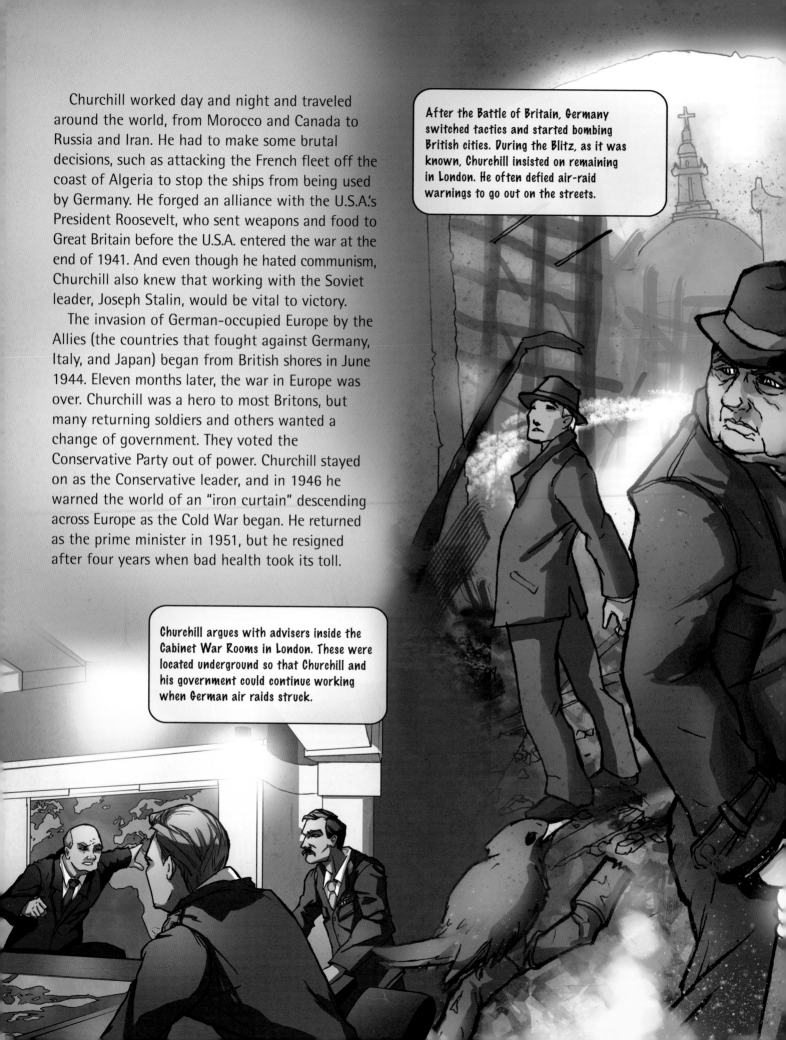

Churchill worked day and night and traveled around the world, from Morocco and Canada to Russia and Iran. He had to make some brutal decisions, such as attacking the French fleet off the coast of Algeria to stop the ships from being used by Germany. He forged an alliance with the U.S.A.'s President Roosevelt, who sent weapons and food to Great Britain before the U.S.A. entered the war at the end of 1941. And even though he hated communism, Churchill also knew that working with the Soviet leader, Joseph Stalin, would be vital to victory.

The invasion of German-occupied Europe by the Allies (the countries that fought against Germany, Italy, and Japan) began from British shores in June 1944. Eleven months later, the war in Europe was over. Churchill was a hero to most Britons, but many returning soldiers and others wanted a change of government. They voted the Conservative Party out of power. Churchill stayed on as the Conservative leader, and in 1946 he warned the world of an "iron curtain" descending across Europe as the Cold War began. He returned as the prime minister in 1951, but he resigned after four years when bad health took its toll.

Churchill argues with advisers inside the Cabinet War Rooms in London. These were located underground so that Churchill and his government could continue working when German air raids struck.

After the Battle of Britain, Germany switched tactics and started bombing British cities. During the Blitz, as it was known, Churchill insisted on remaining in London. He often defied air-raid warnings to go out on the streets.

Churchill discovered a passion for painting soon after he resigned from the government in 1915. More than 570 of his paintings are still in existence today.

Remarkably, Churchill remained an MP until 1964, the year before his death at the age of 90. He was given a state funeral, normally reserved for royalty, which was the largest-ever gathering of world leaders until Pope John Paul II's death in 2005.

Churchill could be a stubborn politician, and he undoubtedly made mistakes. He was often out of step with public opinion, yet he was an extraordinary man with great talents and endless energy. Few people could have stepped into the desperate situation facing Great Britain in 1940, energized an entire country, and led it and its allies to victory five years later.

Churchill views the USS *Augusta*, carrying President Roosevelt in 1941. It would be the first of nine meetings between the two men during World War II.

LIFE LINK

Churchill supported Charles de Gaulle as he tried to establish the Free French Forces, giving de Gaulle access to the BBC (British Broadcasting Corporation) to make radio broadcasts. The stormy relationship between the two men reached a high point on November 11, 1944, when they paraded in triumph through the center of Paris after the city's liberation from the Germans.

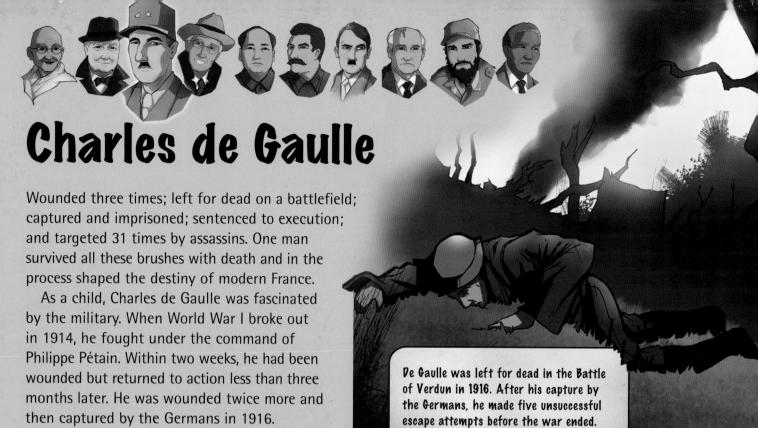

Charles de Gaulle

Wounded three times; left for dead on a battlefield; captured and imprisoned; sentenced to execution; and targeted 31 times by assassins. One man survived all these brushes with death and in the process shaped the destiny of modern France.

As a child, Charles de Gaulle was fascinated by the military. When World War I broke out in 1914, he fought under the command of Philippe Pétain. Within two weeks, he had been wounded but returned to action less than three months later. He was wounded twice more and then captured by the Germans in 1916.

De Gaulle was released in 1918 and fought for the Polish army against Russia. He became a member of France's Supreme War Council, working as Pétain's aide. But in the 1930s he came into conflict with the French military. By the outbreak of World War II in 1939, the tall, extremely confident military man had still not risen above the rank of colonel.

De Gaulle was left for dead in the Battle of Verdun in 1916. After his capture by the Germans, he made five unsuccessful escape attempts before the war ended.

During the war, de Gaulle commanded a tank division against the German invasion. In Caumont he forced the enemy backward, but his success was overshadowed by the general German advance. As France prepared to surrender on July 17, 1940, de Gaulle escaped to Great Britain in disgust. He made the first of many radio broadcasts the next day, urging the French people to continue the war.

De Gaulle had named his son Philippe in honor of Pétain, a hero of World War I. Now the tables had turned. Pétain led France into its surrender and was installed as the leader of the Vichy government— a regime that ruled southern France in collaboration with the Nazis. Pétain's government denounced de Gaulle as a traitor and sentenced him to death in his absence.

De Gaulle argued fiercely with his superiors, who did not agree with his bold plan for a mobile army using tanks and planes.

In May 1940 German forces plowed through Belgium into France, bypassing the Maginot Line of defense that had been built to protect the French border.

The French resistance sabotaged German facilities, smuggled to safety Allied airmen who had been shot down, and gathered vital information for the Allies.

British leader Winston Churchill allowed de Gaulle to make radio broadcasts from London. He ended his first rousing speech with the words, "Whatever happens, the flame of French resistance must not and shall not be extinguished."

In Great Britain, de Gaulle set up the French National Committee of Liberation, or Free French. His tiny band of supporters began to swell. He encouraged resistance inside France and appealed to volunteers from French colonies in Africa and Asia. In 1944, 300,000 Free French participated in the invasion of northern France.

De Gaulle walks in triumph through the streets of Paris, receiving a rapturous welcome after the liberation of the city.

De Gaulle wanted a powerful president to lead France. When this didn't happen, he resigned from the government and formed his own political party in 1947. Support surged and then dwindled for the party, and de Gaulle left politics in 1953. But five years later he was back. The Fourth Republic was in turmoil—it had been led by 15 different prime ministers in 12 years, and its African colony of Algeria was fighting fiercely for independence. De Gaulle was asked to become the first president of the new Fifth Republic in 1958—this time with strong powers.

The president worked hard to make France an independent world power. He negotiated Algeria's freedom, believing it was a war that France could not easily win. As the economy quickly grew, France could afford to develop its own nuclear weapons. De Gaulle refused to allow U.S. missiles to be based on French soil and built up relations with the U.S.S.R. He was one of the first western European leaders to recognize Mao Zedong's communist government in China.

After the Allied forces drove the Germans out of Paris in August 1944, de Gaulle returned home as a hero. He formed a temporary government while France figured out a new constitution (a system of laws for governing a country), which became the Fourth Republic.

The Secret Army Organization (OAS) wanted to keep Algeria as a French colony. It tried to kill de Gaulle several times. In 1962 OAS agents fired at his car in Paris, shooting out its front tire and rear window but failing to hit the president.

In 1968 France was torn apart by strikes, protests, and riots, as young students and workers demanded a new government. Even though de Gaulle's party did well in the elections later that year, he stepped down as president in 1969 and died 18 months later. De Gaulle was a strong-willed man who protected France at all costs. He rallied French resistance against Germany during World War II and helped give his country a major standing on the world stage. He died without wealth but is remembered by many French people as a hero.

Under de Gaulle, France sent satellites into space and built nuclear weapons. It detonated its first hydrogen bomb in 1968.

In May 1968 Paris was shaken by student demonstrations and workers' strikes. Some of the protests turned into bloody battles with armed riot police, causing chaos.

De Gaulle meets the leader of West Germany, Konrad Adenauer (right). De Gaulle strengthened France's relations with West Germany during the 1960s.

LIFE LINK
Even though many of de Gaulle's Free French Forces were equipped by the U.S.A., President Franklin Delano Roosevelt recognized the Vichy government, not the Free French. He left de Gaulle out of wartime conferences and military plans and tried to get his rival, Henri Giraud, installed as France's leader.

Franklin Delano Roosevelt

August 10, 1921. Franklin Delano Roosevelt was sailing his yacht off the coast of Canada when he noticed a small fire on Campobello Island. Leaping ashore, he and his children beat out the flames before jogging 2 mi. (3km) to a pond for a swim before dinner. Back at their 34-room vacation home, FDR, as he was nicknamed, suddenly felt very tired and clambered slowly upstairs to bed. He awoke— in great pain and with a high fever—to find that his legs were paralyzed. At the age of 39, he had contracted the disease polio. His career as a politician and businessman seemed to be over.

Roosevelt was a popular student at Harvard University, where he edited the student newspaper and played football.

Louis McHenry Howe (right) was a tough newspaper reporter who masterminded Roosevelt's election campaigns from 1912 onward. Howe would be a loyal adviser to the man he called "the boss" until Howe's death in 1936.

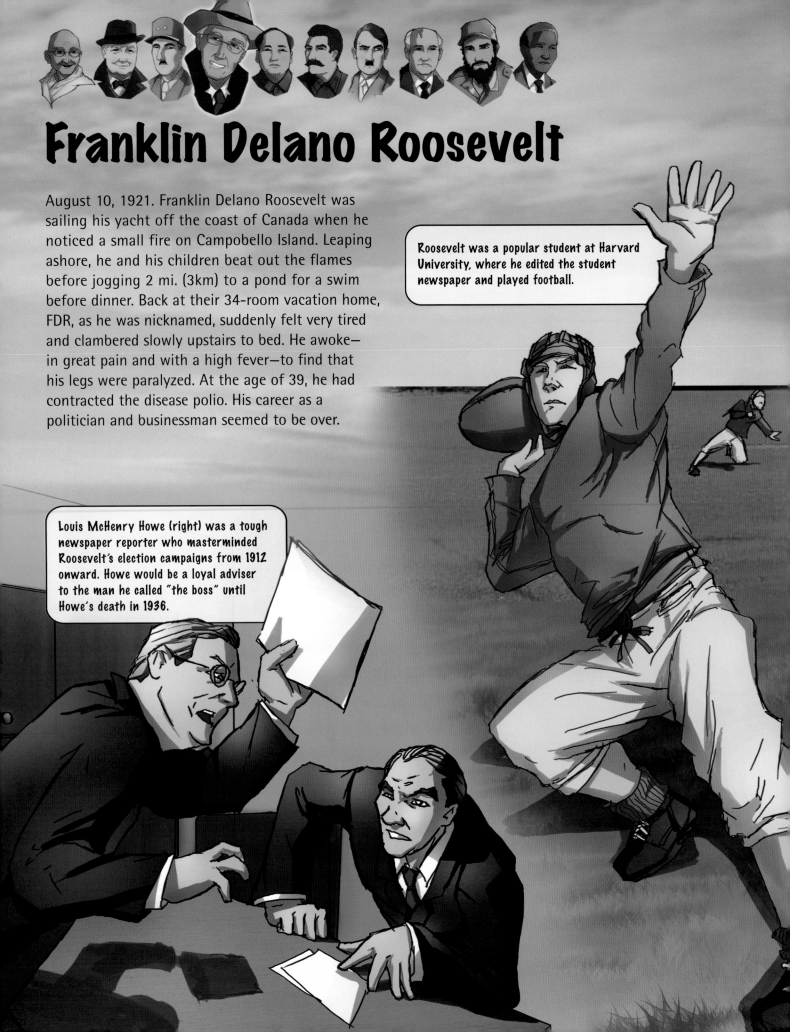

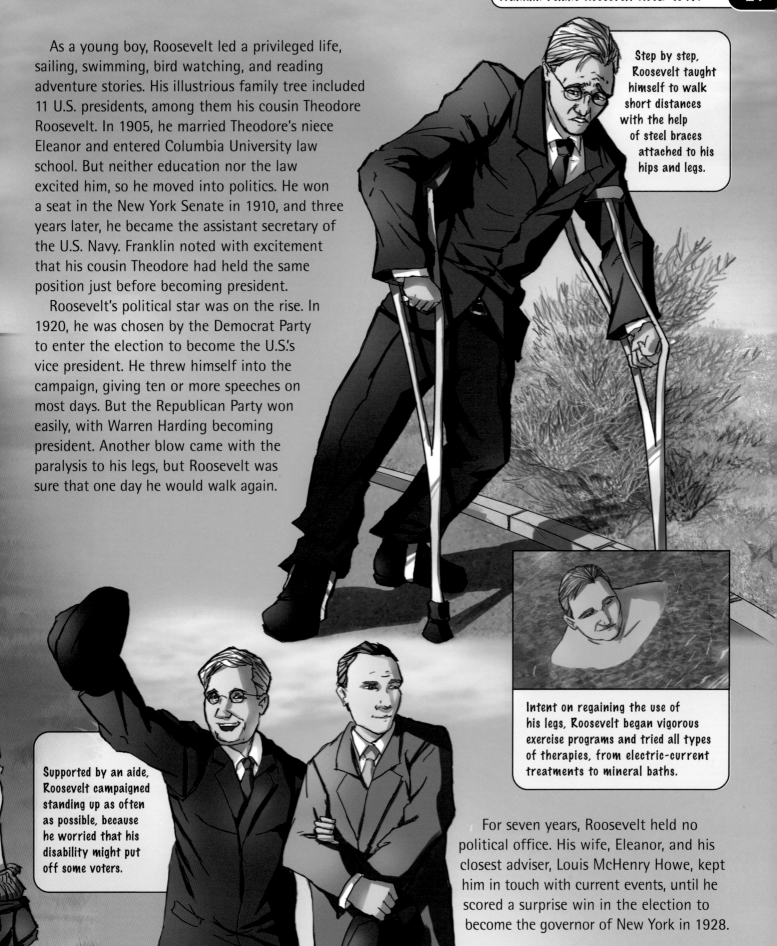

As a young boy, Roosevelt led a privileged life, sailing, swimming, bird watching, and reading adventure stories. His illustrious family tree included 11 U.S. presidents, among them his cousin Theodore Roosevelt. In 1905, he married Theodore's niece Eleanor and entered Columbia University law school. But neither education nor the law excited him, so he moved into politics. He won a seat in the New York Senate in 1910, and three years later, he became the assistant secretary of the U.S. Navy. Franklin noted with excitement that his cousin Theodore had held the same position just before becoming president.

Roosevelt's political star was on the rise. In 1920, he was chosen by the Democrat Party to enter the election to become the U.S.'s vice president. He threw himself into the campaign, giving ten or more speeches on most days. But the Republican Party won easily, with Warren Harding becoming president. Another blow came with the paralysis to his legs, but Roosevelt was sure that one day he would walk again.

Step by step, Roosevelt taught himself to walk short distances with the help of steel braces attached to his hips and legs.

Intent on regaining the use of his legs, Roosevelt began vigorous exercise programs and tried all types of therapies, from electric-current treatments to mineral baths.

Supported by an aide, Roosevelt campaigned standing up as often as possible, because he worried that his disability might put off some voters.

For seven years, Roosevelt held no political office. His wife, Eleanor, and his closest adviser, Louis McHenry Howe, kept him in touch with current events, until he scored a surprise win in the election to become the governor of New York in 1928.

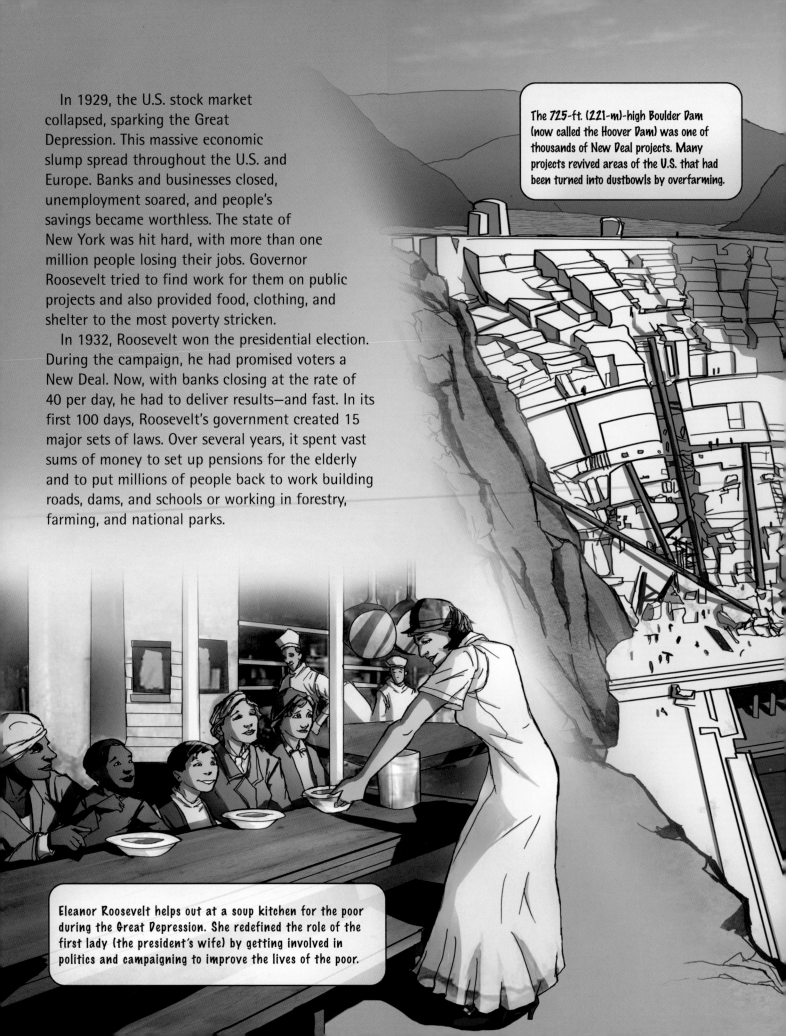

In 1929, the U.S. stock market collapsed, sparking the Great Depression. This massive economic slump spread throughout the U.S. and Europe. Banks and businesses closed, unemployment soared, and people's savings became worthless. The state of New York was hit hard, with more than one million people losing their jobs. Governor Roosevelt tried to find work for them on public projects and also provided food, clothing, and shelter to the most poverty stricken.

In 1932, Roosevelt won the presidential election. During the campaign, he had promised voters a New Deal. Now, with banks closing at the rate of 40 per day, he had to deliver results—and fast. In its first 100 days, Roosevelt's government created 15 major sets of laws. Over several years, it spent vast sums of money to set up pensions for the elderly and to put millions of people back to work building roads, dams, and schools or working in forestry, farming, and national parks.

The 725-ft. (221-m)-high Boulder Dam (now called the Hoover Dam) was one of thousands of New Deal projects. Many projects revived areas of the U.S. that had been turned into dustbowls by overfarming.

Eleanor Roosevelt helps out at a soup kitchen for the poor during the Great Depression. She redefined the role of the first lady (the president's wife) by getting involved in politics and campaigning to improve the lives of the poor.

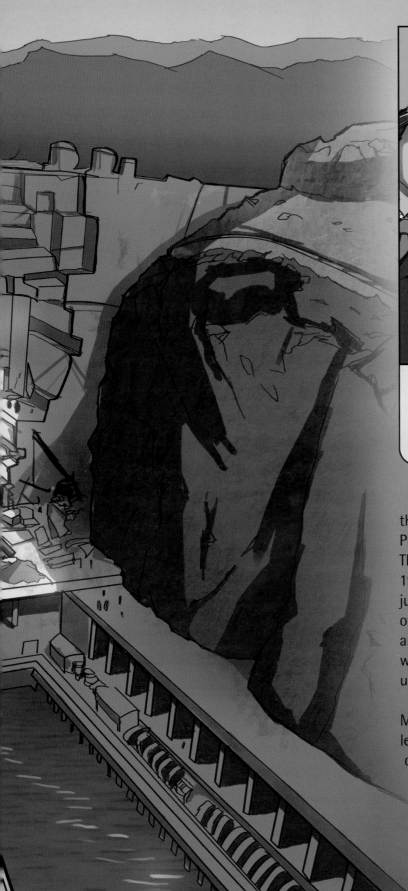

During a parade in Miami, Florida, in 1933, Roosevelt was fired at by Giuseppe Zangara. The assassin, teetering on a wobbly chair to get a clear shot, missed his target. Instead, he hit the mayor of Chicago, Anton Cermak, who died three weeks later.

Roosevelt and his group of advisers, nicknamed the Brain Trust, drew up many of the new laws. Previously, the U.S. Congress had performed this task. The change led to criticism, which grew in the late 1930s when FDR tried to fill the Supreme Court with judges who were more likely to agree with him. Some of the New Deal policies worked well, creating jobs and better living conditions for many people. Others were less successful, and the U.S. still had high unemployment by the early 1940s.

Roosevelt's popularity, however, remained high. Many Americans loved their president's energetic leadership. They reelected him with a huge 61 percent of the vote in 1936 and again in 1940 and 1944. This made him the only U.S. president in history to be elected four times—since 1951, presidents can serve no more than two terms.

Following the end of World War I, the U.S. tried to avoid becoming involved in other nations' affairs. When World War II began in 1939, few Americans wanted to enter another major conflict, so Roosevelt tried to offer aid to Great Britain and its allies without actually going to war.

The U.S. Congress had forbidden arms from being sold to nations at war. Roosevelt found a way around this law in 1940. He exchanged 50 U.S. Navy destroyers for British land in the Caribbean on which to build air bases. As the war raged in Europe, support grew in the U.S. to help Great Britain and its allies. The Lend-Lease Act of 1941 allowed Roosevelt to lend aid, arms, and food and to accept repayment in any form. By the war's end, around $490 million had been granted to some 40 nations, mostly to Great Britain and the Soviet Union.

Roosevelt and Howe quickly realized the power of the media in spreading the president's messages directly to the public. FDR broadcast around 30 "fireside chats" over the radio, helping Americans feel close to their president.

Japan's attack on the naval base of Pearl Harbor, in Hawaii, took the U.S. by surprise. Around 350 aircraft, plus a small number of submarines, devastated the U.S. Pacific fleet. FDR declared war on Japan the next day.

The Japanese raid on Pearl Harbor, in Hawaii, in December 1941 triggered the U.S.'s entry into World War II. Factories churned out vast amounts of arms, and by mid-1943, 12 million Americans had joined the military. The public feared Japan, but FDR insisted that the U.S. should concentrate its military efforts in Europe.

The war took its toll on FDR. In February 1945, a trip to Yalta (in the Ukraine) to meet Joseph Stalin and Winston Churchill exhausted him. On April 12, while posing for a portrait, the president complained of a "terrific headache." They were his last words before losing consciousness. Two and a half hours later, FDR was dead.

The Big Three—Stalin, Roosevelt, and Churchill—met at the Tehran Conference in 1943 and in Yalta in 1945 to discuss how the world would be organized after World War II.

Many people disagreed with some of FDR's economic and wartime decisions, but few contest the fact that he was an honest, highly intelligent statesman who guided his country through two of its greatest challenges—the Great Depression and World War II—and did a lot to improve the lives of millions of ordinary Americans.

LIFE LINK
F. D. Roosevelt sent arms and money to Chiang Kai-shek, who was Mao Zedong's rival in the Chinese Civil War. Roosevelt believed that Chiang would use the weapons to fight Japan. Instead, Chiang used them against Mao's forces. Mao did not forget FDR's support for his enemy, and he refused to meet any U.S. president until 1972.

Mao Zedong

"I lament the fact that for several thousand years the wisdom of the people has not been developed and the country has been teetering on the brink of a grievous disaster." These words were written by Mao Zedong in 1912. China was the world's oldest continuous civilization, but its time-honored ways of government had failed many millions of people who stood on the brink of starvation and rebellion.

As a young boy, Mao worked on the farm of his mother's family. He collected fodder to feed the pigs and led the buffalo to water.

Life was hard for Mao in Peking. During the winter, he spent hours in the library, which was warmer than his freezing home.

Contrary to later propaganda, Mao was not born into a poor peasant family. His father was a successful grain dealer in Hunan province, where Mao went to school before working as a farm hand from the age of 13. Then, hungry for more education, he rebelled against his family and went to study in Changsha, the capital of Hunan. Soon after he arrived, a rebellion broke out, and Mao joined a unit of the revolutionary army that would overthrow China's last emperor.

In 1918, Mao left Hunan for the first time. He traveled to Peking (now Beijing) and found a job at the university library. Mao read many books and was greatly influenced by the chief librarian, Li Dazhao, who was one of the founders of the Chinese Communist Party (CCP). Mao was present at the CCP's first Congress meeting in 1921. Two years later, the communists formed an alliance with the Kuomintang—the nationalist party led by Sun Yat-sen. Soon Mao was an important figure on Kuomintang committees, and he became more and more interested in how ordinary peasants in the country could be inspired and guided to achieve a revolution.

While hiding, Mao's communist troops made their base in a misty forest that teemed with monkeys, snakes, and boars. They lived as bandits, stealing food from nearby villages.

To secure control of the Kuomintang, Chiang Kai-shek (right) ordered his soldiers to arrest many communists in the city of Shanghai (above).

After Sun Yat-sen's death, Chiang Kai-shek became the leader of the Kuomintang. Soon the nationalists and communists were fighting one another. Chiang feared that the communists were becoming too powerful. In 1927, he expelled all communists from his party and began to attack and kill them. Mao and many communists went into hiding, organizing resistance and building support in some parts of China. A key stronghold was Jiangxi Soviet, an area in Jiangxi and Fujian provinces where the communists developed a large peasant army.

Chiang's forces tried to destroy Jiangxi Soviet several times. Finally, in 1934, the communists broke through enemy lines and began the Long March away from danger, with Mao as one of their leaders. They marched up to 50 mi. (80km) every day for one year, crossed 18 mountain ranges, fought off nationalist troops, and suffered starvation and disease. Finally, in October 1935, they set up safe headquarters in Yenan. As news of their feats spread, support for them grew.

In 1937, Japan invaded China. Chiang was forced into an uneasy alliance with the communists in order to defend the country. The communists split their forces into small units, used guerrilla warfare, and were much more successful at fighting the Japanese than the nationalists. The communists spread throughout most of China, recruiting more peasants to their cause. By 1945, Japan had been defeated and the communist forces numbered between 500,000 and 900,000. Tens of millions of peasants supported the party.

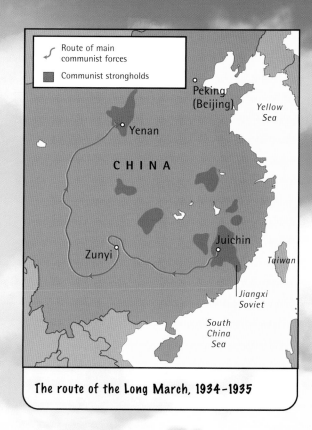

The route of the Long March, 1934-1935

Between 85,000 and 100,000 communists set out on the Long March. No more than 28,000, and possibly as few as 8,000, reached the safety of Shaanxi province.

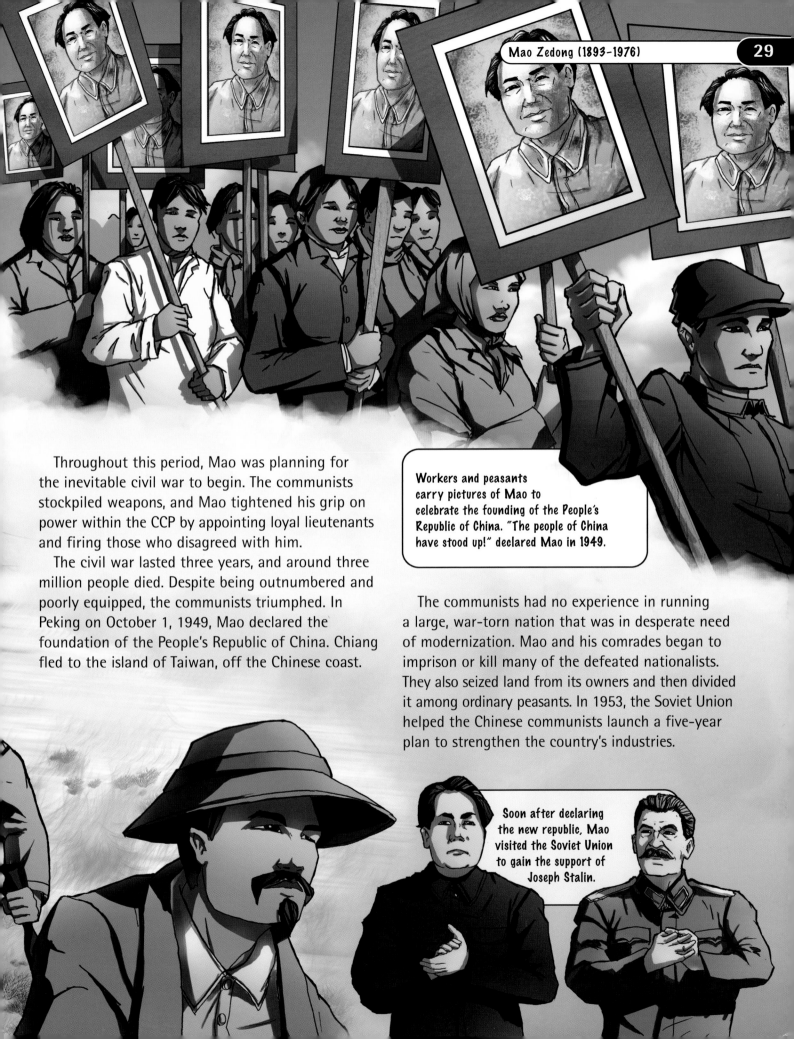

Throughout this period, Mao was planning for the inevitable civil war to begin. The communists stockpiled weapons, and Mao tightened his grip on power within the CCP by appointing loyal lieutenants and firing those who disagreed with him.

The civil war lasted three years, and around three million people died. Despite being outnumbered and poorly equipped, the communists triumphed. In Peking on October 1, 1949, Mao declared the foundation of the People's Republic of China. Chiang fled to the island of Taiwan, off the Chinese coast.

Workers and peasants carry pictures of Mao to celebrate the founding of the People's Republic of China. "The people of China have stood up!" declared Mao in 1949.

The communists had no experience in running a large, war-torn nation that was in desperate need of modernization. Mao and his comrades began to imprison or kill many of the defeated nationalists. They also seized land from its owners and then divided it among ordinary peasants. In 1953, the Soviet Union helped the Chinese communists launch a five-year plan to strengthen the country's industries.

Soon after declaring the new republic, Mao visited the Soviet Union to gain the support of Joseph Stalin.

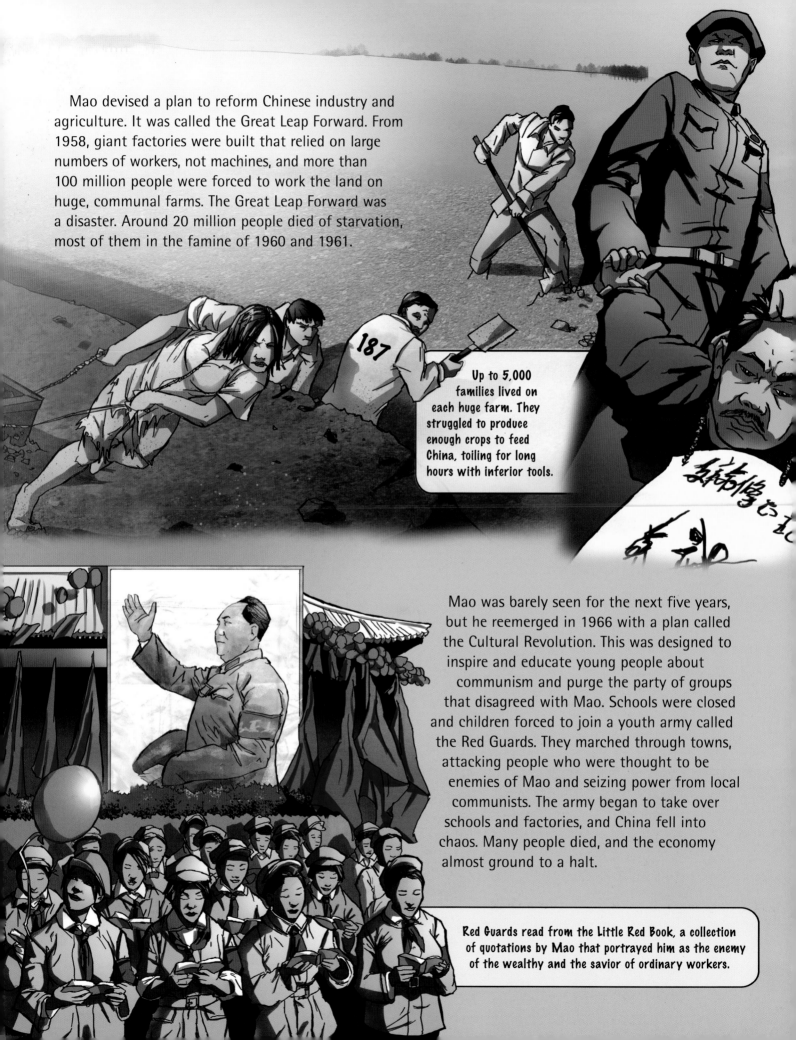

Mao devised a plan to reform Chinese industry and agriculture. It was called the Great Leap Forward. From 1958, giant factories were built that relied on large numbers of workers, not machines, and more than 100 million people were forced to work the land on huge, communal farms. The Great Leap Forward was a disaster. Around 20 million people died of starvation, most of them in the famine of 1960 and 1961.

Up to 5,000 families lived on each huge farm. They struggled to produce enough crops to feed China, toiling for long hours with inferior tools.

Mao was barely seen for the next five years, but he reemerged in 1966 with a plan called the Cultural Revolution. This was designed to inspire and educate young people about communism and purge the party of groups that disagreed with Mao. Schools were closed and children forced to join a youth army called the Red Guards. They marched through towns, attacking people who were thought to be enemies of Mao and seizing power from local communists. The army began to take over schools and factories, and China fell into chaos. Many people died, and the economy almost ground to a halt.

Red Guards read from the Little Red Book, a collection of quotations by Mao that portrayed him as the enemy of the wealthy and the savior of ordinary workers.

By the 1970s, Mao was old and frail. Behind his back, a power struggle began. It was won by Deng Xaoping, a veteran of the Long March. When Mao died in 1976, Deng began to rebuild China's economy and forge stronger links with countries in the West.

During the Cultural Revolution, anyone who did not support Mao became a target. Intellectuals were humiliated in public (left), had their hair hacked off (right), or were robbed and tortured.

Myths surround Mao to this day. Some of his heroic feats, such as leading a charge across a rickety suspension bridge at the height of a battle during the Long March, are now believed not to have happened. Some people revere Mao as the man who united his country when it was in danger of falling apart, securing China's independence. But many more remember him as a ruthless oppressor of religious and cultural groups whose disastrous experiments with the economy caused millions of people to die.

Liu Shaoqi had been in line to succeed Mao, but he was expelled from the Communist Party during the Cultural Revolution.

The Gang of Four was a group led by Jiang Qing (right), Mao's wife. They wielded a great deal of influence during the Cultural Revolution but failed to take power after Mao's death.

LIFE LINK
The Chinese Communist Party was greatly influenced by Joseph Stalin, the leader of the Soviet Union from the late 1920s. Mao's first journey overseas was to Moscow in 1949, where he attended Stalin's 70th birthday celebrations.

Joseph Stalin

To his devoted mother, he was Soso; to his classmates, he was Pocky because of his smallpox-scarred skin; and to rivals in the Soviet Communist Party, he was known as Comrade Card Index thanks to his role in organization, administration, and paperwork. But history remembers him with the name he took for himself in his 30s—Stalin, meaning "man of steel."

Joseph Stalin was born Iosif Dzhugashvili in Gori, Georgia, which was part of the Russian empire and ruled by a kinglike czar. He was sent to a parochial school and forced to learn Russian instead of his native Georgian language. Many of his classmates came from wealthier families than him. They mocked his halting Russian, poverty, and scarred face . . . but not for long. Stalin was a tough adversary in the playground and a bright student with an incredible memory. He graduated first in his class in 1894 and won a place at a theological seminary—a school where students train to become priests— in Tiflis (now Tbilisi), the capital of Georgia.

Stalin's father was a poor shoemaker who was forced to work in a shoe factory after his own business failed. He was sometimes violent, beating his wife and son during drunken rages.

Stalin was a fiery student at the seminary, where he argued with the priests, read banned books, and discussed politics.

Stalin met Lenin for the first time in 1905, at a communist conference held in Finland.

Life at the seminary was strict, but Stalin broke the rules by secretly reading banned books. One of them was *The Communist Manifesto*, cowritten by the philosopher Karl Marx. Marx's writings had a great impact on Stalin, who joined the revolutionary Russian Social-Democratic Workers' Party (RSDLP) after he was expelled from the seminary in 1899.

Stalin devoted his energy to the struggle for a communist revolution. He wrote pamphlets, made speeches, and organized demonstrations. He changed his name and identity in an attempt to elude the czar's secret police, the Okhrana, but was arrested seven or eight times between 1902 and 1913.

After his first arrest, Stalin was exiled to Siberia in late 1903. He soon escaped and began to encourage more protests and strikes upon his return to Tiflis.

The RSDLP split into two groups—the Mensheviks and the more radical Bolsheviks, led by Vladimir Lenin. In 1912, Lenin promoted Stalin to the editor of the Bolshevik Party newspaper, *Pravda*. The following year, betrayed by a double agent, Stalin was arrested again. This time he was sent to one of the remotest parts of Siberia for life.

Stalin organized "fighting squads" that raided banks and steamships in order to provide money for the communists. In 1907, his gang attacked a bank stagecoach in Tiflis town square, throwing bombs before stealing more than 250,000 rubles—a huge fortune.

A revolution in spring 1917 overthrew the czar as the ruler of Russia. Political prisoners were released, including Stalin. A second revolution in the fall was followed by a civil war, from which the Bolsheviks emerged triumphant. In 1922, they founded the Union of Soviet Socialist Republics (U.S.S.R.), or Soviet Union, with Lenin as its leader.

Stalin used his power as the general secretary to expel his great rival Leon Trotsky (left) from the Soviet Union in 1929. Trotsky was later assassinated in Mexico on Stalin's orders.

Stalin rose through the ranks during the war to become the general secretary of the Communist Party (the renamed Bolshevik Party). The position seemed minor, but it allowed him to give party jobs to his allies and to build his own power base.

When Lenin died in 1924, Stalin plotted cleverly. He portrayed himself as Lenin's greatest follower and pitted his rivals against one another. One by one, his opponents were removed from power. By the late 1920s, Stalin was in almost total control and ruled as a dictator.

Bolsheviks stormed the Winter Palace in Saint Petersburg during the 1917 October Revolution. They met little resistance and overthrew Russia's provisional government.

Russia had long been in need of modernization. Stalin wanted to create a mighty, self-sufficient nation, so he forced the Soviet Union to build up its heavy industries such as coal mining and the manufacturing of steel, machinery, tractors, and railroad and military equipment. Five-Year Plans set high targets for every region, factory, mine, and even for each individual worker.

Stalin ordered farmers to band together to form huge farms under state control, known as collectives. The idea was that these farms could use new scientific methods and machinery to boost food production. But many peasants destroyed their crops and animals in protest. Thousands of people were executed or sent to labor camps. Their lands were seized, and food shortages struck the countryside. Famines in 1932 and 1933 caused millions of deaths.

By 1934, many people wanted Sergey Kirov, a civil war hero, to take over from Stalin. But when Kirov was murdered, Stalin used his death as an excuse to launch a series of show trials that became known as the Great Purge.

Many people were forced to move to factory and mining areas. Workers who failed to meet their targets were fined or beaten, arrested, or sent to labor camps known as gulags.

Stalin tried to wipe out the wealthier peasant farmers, or kulaks. Most were either executed, sent to gulags, or banished to live in barren wastelands.

Thousands of people, from farmers to army officials, were arrested by the secret police in the Great Purge.

At a series of show trials in Moscow, Communist Party members were found guilty of plotting against Stalin.

Most of the people found guilty died or were sentenced to hard labor in gulags in the barren north and east.

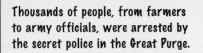

The goal of the Great Purge was to remove Stalin's opponents in the Communist Party and the military. But it spread to almost all levels of society. The dreaded NKVD secret police terrorized the Soviet people, encouraging them to betray their neighbors and families. Up to one third of the Red Army's officers were executed, leaving the military short of leaders as World War II broke out. At first this was not a problem because the Soviet Union and Germany had agreed not to fight each other while Stalin's forces occupied Estonia, Latvia, Lithuania, and parts of Poland and Romania.

But when Germany invaded the Soviet Union in 1941, Stalin had to join the Allies. The Soviets fought bitterly and were sacrificed in their millions by Stalin. The decisive battle was fought in the city of Stalingrad (now Volgograd) from August 1942 to February 1943. Around 1.5 million people died, but the Germans were forced to retreat.

Stalin drove a hard bargain with Winston Churchill and F. D. Roosevelt, extending Soviet influence over most of Eastern Europe. Within three years after the end of the war, communist governments supported by the Soviet Union were running Poland, Hungary, Romania, Bulgaria, and Czechoslovakia. In 1949, East Germany became a communist state, separate from the western, capitalist part of Germany.

Stalin had giant statues of himself put up throughout the Soviet Union. They portrayed him as a heroic, mighty leader who dominated the lives of his people.

In his 70s, Stalin's health began to fail. He became more and more paranoid. In March 1953, he dined with some of his most senior ministers. Stalin fell ill and died shortly afterward. Rumors soon spread that one or more of the diners might have poisoned him.

Stalin was a cunning, ruthless leader who drove the Soviet Union to develop its industries, repel Adolf Hitler's armies, and emerge after World War II as one of the world's two superpowers, along with the U.S. But his successes came at a terrible cost. The rights and freedoms of the Soviets were crushed in an atmosphere of terror, and the Great Purge and other policies led to the deaths of more than 20 million people.

On April 30, 1945, a soldier from the Soviet Red Army waves his country's flag over the Reichstag parliament building in Berlin. Germany surrendered one week later.

LIFE LINK
Joseph Stalin and Adolf Hitler never met, but their foreign ministers signed a nonaggression pact in 1939. Hitler's decision to invade the Soviet Union in 1941 was a turning point in the war, which ended with Stalin's forces reaching Berlin, Germany, and prompting Hitler to commit suicide.

Adolf Hitler

July 20, 1944. Colonel Claus von Stauffenberg set down his briefcase next to Adolf Hitler, mumbled his apologies, and left the hut in the war headquarters of Rastenberg, Germany. Field Marshal Wilhelm Keitel was furious, but Hitler nodded his approval. Everyone knew how much the German dictator admired the brave and intelligent colonel. Seconds later, the case exploded. The bomb ripped through the hut, killing four men. But the plot by von Stauffenberg and other senior soldiers to murder their terrifying leader had failed. Hitler survived.

Von Stauffenberg flees as his bomb explodes. Hitler was injured and took revenge on the plotters. As many as 4,900 people were executed.

After his small inheritance ran out, Hitler endured a hard winter in 1909. People ignored him when he begged, until he was forced to find shelter in a hostel for Vienna's homeless.

Adolf Hitler was born in the Austrian town of Braunau am Inn, on the border with Germany. His father, a customs official named Alois, was strict. His mother, Klara, doted on and spoiled him. Hitler did badly at school, left without graduating, and was labeled lazy and disobedient by his teachers.

In 1907, he moved to Vienna, Austria, where he dreamed of becoming a painter but failed to gain a place at the Academy of Fine Arts. Penniless, Hitler lived on the streets, ate in soup kitchens, and shoveled snow or begged for money. He finally made a living as a painter by copying postcards and scenes of Vienna, before moving to Munich, Germany, in 1913. One year later, he failed a medical assessment for the Austro-Hungarian army, but he was accepted into a German infantry regiment instead.

Hitler painted dozens of scenes of Vienna, but he was not happy in the city because he detested its mix of different cultures. Many people believe that his hatred of Jewish people began at this time.

During World War I, Hitler worked as a runner, with the dangerous job of delivering messages between command posts. He was awarded the Iron Cross medal but failed to climb the ranks because he was thought of as a loner.

In 1918, Hitler went temporarily blind after a poisonous gas attack by British forces in Ypres (now Ieper, Belgium). As he recovered, he heard the news of Germany's surrender.

After Germany's humiliating defeat at the end of World War I, threats of a communist revolution were in the air. Hitler believed that the German army had been betrayed by Jews and other peoples he considered to be inferior. In 1919, he joined the German Workers' Party, a small group of extremists who were fiercely anticommunist and anti-Jewish. Hitler discovered that he had a gift for powerful public speaking. Fueled by his fury at Germany's surrender, he began to build a loyal following. By 1921, he was effectively the leader of the party, which had been renamed the National Socialist German Workers' Party, or Nazi Party.

In 1923, Hitler tried to seize power in southern Germany. It went very wrong. He was sent to prison, where he wrote *Mein Kampf* (*My Struggle*), a book that outlined his belief in the superiority of the German people, especially Aryans (white, blond-haired, blue-eyed people). Following his release, Hitler found that he was banned from making speeches. Support for the Nazi Party faded, but this did not stop him from building a network of local parties throughout Germany.

The late 1920s were difficult years for the Nazis, until Germany lurched into a crisis following the 1929 Wall Street Crash. U.S. loans that bolstered the German economy were withdrawn. Unemployment and poverty soared, alongside a surge in support for extreme political parties. The Nazis whipped up hysteria against their rivals with a mixture of brutal bullying and sophisticated propaganda. In the first of two elections in 1932, they won more than 13 million votes, more than one third of the poll.

In prison, Hitler dictated *Mein Kampf* to Rudolf Hess, a fellow Nazi. The book blamed Germany's problems on Jews and urged the German people to rise up and destroy communism and democracy.

Hitler's attempt to seize power in 1923 is known as the Beer Hall Putsch, or coup. He led around 2,500 armed men into Munich and then burst into a political meeting at a beer hall. The police, who were well prepared for their arrival, foiled the uprising quickly.

Key Nazis included Joseph Goebbels (left), who was in charge of propaganda, Hermann Göring (second left), the head of the air force, and Heinrich Himmler (right), the leader of the secret police.

Hitler used the support that the Nazis had won to plot his path to power. He joined forces with important politicians who hated communism and thought that Hitler could be controlled. They were wrong. Hitler was made chancellor of Germany in January 1933. One month later, the Reichstag parliament building burned down. The fire was blamed on communists and used as an excuse to give Hitler emergency powers. The Nazi takeover was fast and brutal. Hitler had hundreds of rivals killed during the Night of the Long Knives in June 1934. In August, he declared himself führer (absolute leader) of the Third Reich, or German Empire.

Hitler knew how to make people listen to him. His powerful speeches hammered home simple messages such as how Germany had been betrayed by Jews.

Hitler set to work rebuilding Germany's economy and pride. Large public projects provided jobs for millions of people, and huge rallies were organized to praise Hitler. But at the same time, minority groups were oppressed, and criticism was stamped out by the SS (*Schutzstaffel*) (protection squad) and the Gestapo secret police. And all the while, Hitler was preparing for war.

The SS was set up to protect Hitler, but it also terrorized ordinary Germans and crushed any dissent in the Nazi Party.

Germany organized the biggest military buildup that the world had ever seen and began to expand its territory. In 1936, it reclaimed the Rhineland area, which had been lost after World War I; in 1938, Austria was forced to join with Germany; and in September 1939, Hitler invaded Poland, triggering the start of World War II.

Throughout the 1930s, Jews were violently attacked, had their belongings stolen, and began to be sent to prisonlike concentration camps.

Mainland northern Europe was under German occupation in less than one year, but a plan to invade Great Britain was abandoned. Instead, German airplanes began bombing raids on Great Britain while Hitler switched fronts to invade the Soviet Union. The German army powered deep into enemy territory, but a bitter defeat at the Battle of Stalingrad saw the Soviets repel Hitler's forces. Coupled with the U.S.'s entry into the war, Italy's surrender in 1943, and the Allies' invasion of northern France in 1944, the tide of the war turned against Hitler and Germany.

Hitler awards medals to some of the most devoted members of the Hitler Youth. By 1940, this organization had eight million members. As the war turned against Germany, members as young as 12 were forced to fight and die for their country.

Hitler invaded the Soviet Union in order to crush communism and create lebensraum (living space) for German settlers, but his exhausted troops were defeated in Stalingrad (now Volgograd) in 1943.

On January 30, 1945, Hitler made his final radio broadcast to the German people from his bunker in Berlin. By April, Russian tanks had rumbled into the city. Sick, exhausted, and finally admitting defeat, Hitler married his girlfriend, Eva Braun, on April 29 and sent away his beloved dog, Blondi, to be poisoned. The next day, he and Eva committed suicide.

Hitler's legacy is the shocking death toll from World War II and the Nazis' extermination of peoples they considered inferior. Hitler ordered the killing of three million non-Jewish Poles, almost as many Soviet prisoners of war, Romany peoples, and the disabled. He fueled violence and hatred that led to the deaths of around six million Jews through starvation, disease, and mass executions—an act of genocide known as the Holocaust. In the words of one survivor, Hitler left his mark on the world as the "incarnation of absolute evil."

Jews from all over Europe were sent to extermination camps run by the SS, where they were murdered, mostly in poison gas chambers.

Hitler lived and worked in his underground bunker in Berlin from late 1944. He became more and more unpredictable, exhausted, and isolated and had to fight off several attempts by his officers to wrestle control from him.

LIFE LINK
Hitler's corpse was captured by the Soviet army and buried in Magdeburg, East Germany. In 1970, Yuri Andropov, the head of the KGB (the Soviet Union's central intelligence agency), ordered the body to be dug up, cremated, and the ashes scattered. Andropov later had Mikhail Gorbachev promoted to the leader of the Soviet Communist Party.

Mikhail Gorbachev

September 19, 1978. Four men stood on a narrow railroad platform in Mineralnye Vody, an isolated location 1,116 mi. (1,800km) from Moscow. Mikhail Gorbachev, the governor of the local Stavropol province, was introduced to the president of his country, Leonid Brezhnev, and his deputy, Konstantin Chernenko. Making the introductions was Yuri Andropov, the head of the feared spy and secret police agency, the KGB. Within weeks, Gorbachev would be whisked off to Moscow to become the secretary for agriculture. And within a decade all four men would have held power as the leader of the Soviet Union.

Gorbachev was born into a poor farming family. After World War II he helped his father operate a combine, before earning a place at Moscow University to study law. Life was hard for the new student, who had to share a room with up to 15 other people. In 1953 his wedding to Raisa Titarenko took place in a corner of the student dining room.

Leonid Brezhnev (left) meets with the three men (Andropov, Chernenko, and Gorbachev) who would succeed him as the last leaders of the Soviet Union.

Gorbachev was 11 years old and living in his family's tiny three-room brick cottage when German tanks rolled into Stavropol in 1942. His father was away, fighting in the Soviet army.

The teenage Gorbachev worked on a large farm through scorching summers and bitterly cold winters. In 1949 he won the prestigious Order of the Red Banner of Labor after helping grow and reap a record harvest.

Gorbachev moved back to Stavropol in 1955 and began to work his way up through the enormous Communist Party organization that ran all aspects of life in the Soviet Union. He was promoted to the position of first secretary of Stavropol in 1970 and governed a region that was home to 2.4 million people.

Gorbachev was a hard-working, honest governor, but he remained almost unknown outside Stavropol until his surprise move to Moscow in 1978. Two years later, at the age of 49, he was promoted to the Politburo—the elite body of around a dozen men who ran the Soviet Union. He was 21 years younger than the average age of its other members.

In the early 1980s Brezhnev, Andropov, and Chernenko all ruled as Soviet leader before their deaths. When Gorbachev came to power in March 1985, the country was in crisis. Its economy had been crippled by corruption, a lack of reform, and the cost of keeping pace with the U.S. in a gigantic arms race. It was also supporting the communist governments of many eastern European countries and fighting an unpopular and costly war in Afghanistan.

Yuri Andropov first met Gorbachev on a visit to the Stavropol mineral baths. The KGB leader became a powerful force in Gorbachev's rise to power.

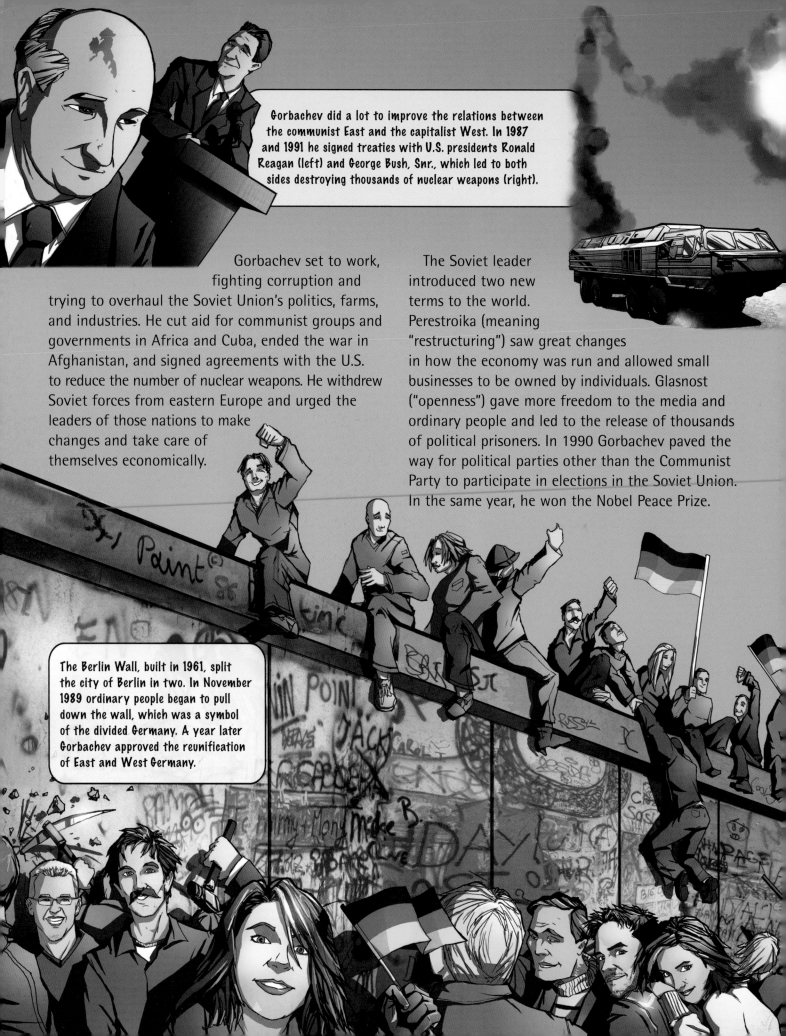

Gorbachev did a lot to improve the relations between the communist East and the capitalist West. In 1987 and 1991 he signed treaties with U.S. presidents Ronald Reagan (left) and George Bush, Snr., which led to both sides destroying thousands of nuclear weapons (right).

Gorbachev set to work, fighting corruption and trying to overhaul the Soviet Union's politics, farms, and industries. He cut aid for communist groups and governments in Africa and Cuba, ended the war in Afghanistan, and signed agreements with the U.S. to reduce the number of nuclear weapons. He withdrew Soviet forces from eastern Europe and urged the leaders of those nations to make changes and take care of themselves economically.

The Soviet leader introduced two new terms to the world. Perestroika (meaning "restructuring") saw great changes in how the economy was run and allowed small businesses to be owned by individuals. Glasnost ("openness") gave more freedom to the media and ordinary people and led to the release of thousands of political prisoners. In 1990 Gorbachev paved the way for political parties other than the Communist Party to participate in elections in the Soviet Union. In the same year, he won the Nobel Peace Prize.

The Berlin Wall, built in 1961, split the city of Berlin in two. In November 1989 ordinary people began to pull down the wall, which was a symbol of the divided Germany. A year later Gorbachev approved the reunification of East and West Germany.

As the Soviet people began to demand more freedom from the ruling Communist Party, violent demonstrations for independence broke out in many Soviet republics.

Praise for Gorbachev from abroad could not mask the turmoil at home. Some reforms failed, the economy struggled, and severe food shortages struck. Several of the 15 republics that made up the Soviet Union were clamoring for independence. In 1991 powerful Soviet figures tried to take over the country. The coup was unsuccessful. Gorbachev fired many politicians and gave more power to the republics, but his position was weakened.

By Christmas Day 1991, it was all over. Gorbachev resigned, and one day later the Soviet Union ceased to exist. In its place were Russia and the other former republics, now independent nations.

Gorbachev's time in power left the world greatly changed. In Russia he is still viewed critically—when he entered the presidential election in 1996, he won less than 1.5 percent of the vote. Yet abroad he is known as a brave politician who brought freedom to eastern Europe and an end to the Cold War.

Gorbachev was arrested at his vacation home during the 1991 coup, which was led by the communist heads of the army, police, and KGB.

Politician Boris Yeltsin called on the army to withdraw its tanks. When some troops switched sides, the coup collapsed.

LIFE LINK
In 1989 Mikhail Gorbachev told Fidel Castro that the Soviet Union would be cutting the aid that it sent to Cuba. Two years later KGB director Vladimir Kryuchkov and General Nicolai Leonov held secret talks with Castro. Within weeks, both men would be ringleaders of the 1991 coup against Gorbachev.

Fidel Castro

August 5, 1951. Partway through his weekly radio broadcast, Eddy Chibás, the leader of Cuba's main opposition party, the Ortodoxo, raised a gun and shot himself. His suicide was intended to alert the Cuban people to the economic plight of their country and the corruption of its leaders. It left a power vacuum in his party that a fiery young lawyer, Fidel Castro Ruz, tried to fill . . .

As a boy, Castro loved climbing mountains and hunting. He was also a natural speechmaker, with an interest in politics. He once tried to persuade the workers at his father's sugar plantation to rise up and demand better treatment. In 1947, at the age of 21, he joined a band of rebels in a failed attempt to invade the Dominican Republic and overthrow its dictator, Rafael Trujillo. Three years later he became a lawyer in Havana, where he worked to help some of the city's poorest people.

Castro went to Belen College, one of the best schools in Havana, Cuba's capital. In 1944 he was voted the best athlete in the college.

The plot to overthrow Trujillo was called off before the rebels reached the Dominican Republic. Castro swam several miles through shark-infested waters in order to evade being captured.

Castro planned to capture the Moncada barracks and broadcast to the Cuban people to rise up against Batista. But some of the rebel cars got lost, and the remaining 150 fighters were beaten easily.

At his trial in 1953, Castro set out his vision of a Cuba free from poverty and the interference of foreign countries.

Castro was 26 when he decided to stand for election on behalf of the Ortodoxo Party in 1952. But the election never took place because General Fulgencio Batista seized power. Supported by the U.S., he ruled Cuba as a dictator. In response, Castro assembled a band of rebels to attack the Moncada army barracks on July 26, 1953.

Weeks later, Castro sat in jail at the beginning of a 15-year sentence. The raid had been a disaster. Castro was tried and found guilty. But within two years, he was set free. Castro left for Mexico to form a group called the "July 26th Movement." He recruited exiles from Cuba and Latin America, among them a young Argentinian doctor named Ernesto "Che" Guevara.

Castro and Guevara believed that the only way to topple Batista was to use guerrilla warfare and to win the support of ordinary Cubans. Castro made plans to return to Cuba just as his allies on the island started an uprising.

On November 25, 1956, Castro's rebels set off in a battered, leaking yacht that was designed to hold 12 people. On that night it was crammed with 82 men. By the time they landed, two days late, General Batista's forces were on the alert. Only around a dozen rebels, including Castro, his brother Raúl, and a wounded Che Guevara, made it to the safety of the Sierra Maestra Mountains.

News of Castro's rebels spread. The poor peoples of the Sierra Maestra took care of them. From their mountain base, Castro's growing band could attack Batista's army and then retreat to safety. Unrest grew in the cities as support for Cuba's leader dwindled. By 1958, Castro had united the groups that stood against Batista. The general sent thousands of soldiers to attack the rebels, but a number of his troops switched sides. Castro came close to defeat, but eventually he marched toward Havana in triumph.

The rebels' week-long boat trip from Mexico to Cuba did not go smoothly. On the last night, one of the men fell overboard. Castro risked discovery by turning on the searchlights to rescue him.

After landing on the Cuban coast, the rebels were betrayed by a guide and ambushed by Batista's forces. Most were killed, but Castro and Che Guevara (far left) escaped.

On a 1959 visit to the U.S. Castro met the leaders of Egypt and India, the African-American civil-rights leader Malcolm X, and U.S. Vice President Richard Nixon (above).

The Cuban government took control of American oil refineries on the island. In response, the U.S. refused to buy Cuban sugar, the country's most important crop. Castro then seized American property in Cuba, and the U.S. banned almost all exports to the island.

In April 1961 around 1,500 Cuban exiles, trained by the U.S. Central Intelligence Agency (CIA), landed in the Bay of Pigs on Cuba's coast. Their aim was to overthrow Castro, but they were easily beaten, strengthening the Cuban leader's grip on power. Many Cubans now agreed with Castro's anti-American speeches, but critics of his regime were sent to prison or even executed.

Batista fled on New Year's Day 1959. Many of his supporters were executed, and by February Castro was the prime minister. He was only 32 years old.

Castro knew that Cuba's relationship with the world's two superpowers, the U.S. and the Soviet Union, would be crucial. Almost immediately there was friction between Castro and the Americans.

The Cuban army captured more than 1,000 U.S.-backed troops in the Bay of Pigs. To release them, Castro demanded food and medical supplies worth $53 million.

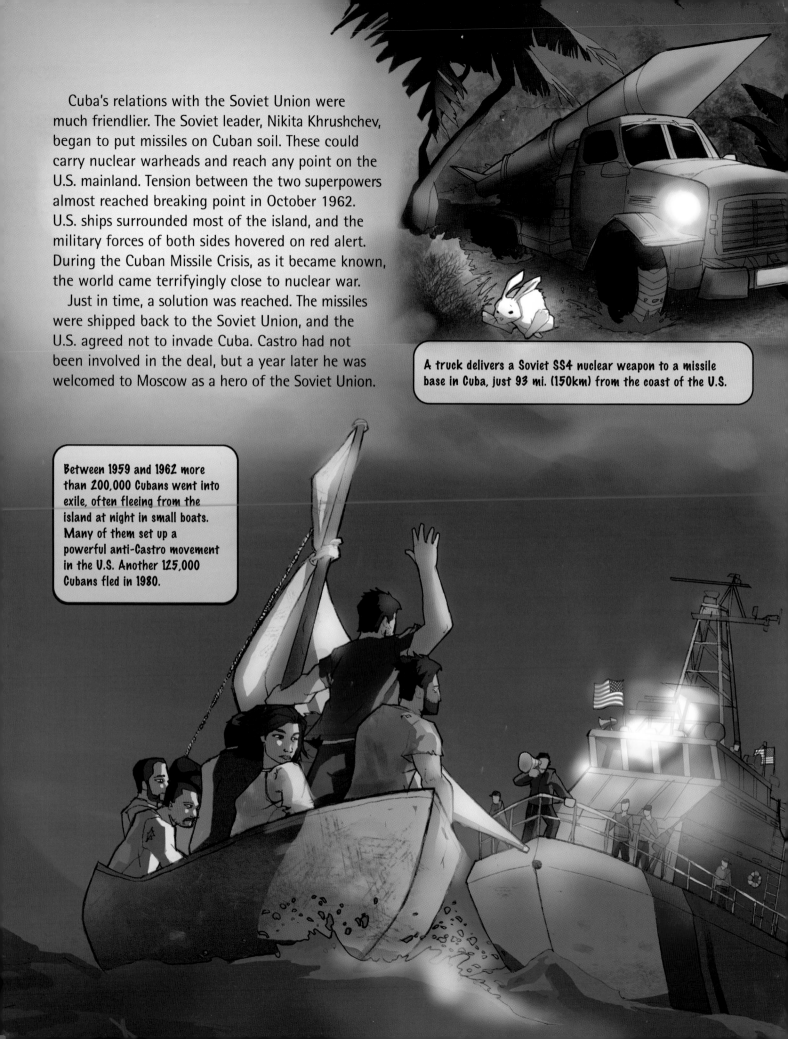

Cuba's relations with the Soviet Union were much friendlier. The Soviet leader, Nikita Khrushchev, began to put missiles on Cuban soil. These could carry nuclear warheads and reach any point on the U.S. mainland. Tension between the two superpowers almost reached breaking point in October 1962. U.S. ships surrounded most of the island, and the military forces of both sides hovered on red alert. During the Cuban Missile Crisis, as it became known, the world came terrifyingly close to nuclear war.

Just in time, a solution was reached. The missiles were shipped back to the Soviet Union, and the U.S. agreed not to invade Cuba. Castro had not been involved in the deal, but a year later he was welcomed to Moscow as a hero of the Soviet Union.

A truck delivers a Soviet SS4 nuclear weapon to a missile base in Cuba, just 93 mi. (150km) from the coast of the U.S.

Between 1959 and 1962 more than 200,000 Cubans went into exile, often fleeing from the island at night in small boats. Many of them set up a powerful anti-Castro movement in the U.S. Another 125,000 Cubans fled in 1980.

From the 1960s Castro sent soldiers and support to communist rebel forces in Angola (below), Ghana, Nicaragua, and Bolivia.

Castro often gave fiery speeches alongside his brother. In 1976 a new constitution made Castro president.

With the help of the Soviet Union, Castro began to change Cuba's way of life in the 1960s. He built a welfare system to provide free education and healthcare. Today, 97 percent of Cuban adults can read and write, and the average life expectancy is 77, equal to the U.S. But these policies put a great strain on the Cuban economy, which reached breaking point when the Soviet Union collapsed in 1991. Soviet aid, worth $6 billion per year, was canceled, and Cuba entered a long economic crisis known as the Special Period in Peacetime, with shortages of food and fuel.

With his health failing, Castro handed power to his brother Raúl in 2008. Around the world he is both loved and hated. He improved conditions for Cuba's poor, but his critics say that he banned democratic elections and sent thousands of people to prison just because they disagreed with him.

For Cuba, it is a time of uncertainty. Fidel Castro held complete power for almost half a century—so long that almost three fourths of Cuban people have known no other leader until now.

One of Castro's most influential friends is Nelson Mandela. But he has made deadly enemies too. There have been more than 600 attempts to kill him, many of them set up by the CIA.

LIFE LINK
Castro has been an inspiration to many people, including Nelson Mandela. Cuba was one of the first countries that Mandela visited after his release from prison. Castro went to South Africa in 1998, when Mandela presented him with the Order of Good Hope, South Africa's highest award for foreigners.

Nelson Mandela

August 5, 1962. Chauffeur David Motsamai was driving toward Johannesburg when a police car sped past and signaled for him to stop. He hid his gun on the floor of the car and eyed the terrain. A railroad embankment on one side might offer an escape route, but the land was unfamiliar. He would be shot within seconds. The South African police were elated—David Motsamai was just an alias. They had caught Nelson Mandela, a man they had been hunting for 17 months.

Rolihlahla Mandela was born in the South African village of Mvezo. After his father died, he went to live with the family of Chief Jongintaba, the leader of the Thembu tribe. Mandela went to a boarding school and then a very good college, Fort Hare, but he was suspended for organizing a strike among the students. Another striker, Oliver Tambo, became his lifelong friend.

> Mandela was captured on his way back from a meeting with the chief of the Xhosa tribe. He had been working undercover for more than a year.

> Mandela became an enthusiastic boxer, sparring and following a grueling training program in order to stay in shape.

Mandela would not apologize to the college and refused a marriage that had been arranged for him by Chief Jongintaba. So he moved to Johannesburg, where he met Walter Sisulu. In 1944 Mandela, Sisulu, and Tambo formed the Youth League of the African National Congress (ANC) political party. Its aim was to organize peaceful protests against the racist South African regime.

> Rolihlahla was seven years old when his teacher gave him the name Nelson on his first day at school.

In 1948 South Africa's policy of apartheid (which means "apartness") was made into law. It involved keeping apart people of different races. Black people and Indians were banned from certain jobs, forbidden from marrying someone of a different race, and even told which buses they could take. Many black people were forced to live in townships outside of the big cities or in rural "homelands." These were usually regions of poor farmland with few facilities or jobs.

Mandela was at the heart of the ANC's Defiance Campaign, in which peaceful protestors disobeyed the apartheid laws. He was often arrested, harassed, and banned from attending meetings. In 1956 he was charged with high treason alongside more than 150 ANC leaders and anti-apartheid campaigners, including Tambo and Sisulu. The trial ran until 1961, when all of them were found not guilty. By that time, Mandela was on the run.

In 1952 Mandela (center) and Tambo (left) opened up a law firm in Johannesburg. They marched in protests and took on the cases of many people persecuted by the apartheid laws.

In 1960 the police killed 67 people during a rally against apartheid in the township of Sharpeville. In the uproar that followed, the ANC was banned.

For several years Mandela and others had debated whether the ANC should take up violent protests. In 1961 they formed a military group to sabotage government facilities and buildings. Mandela was its commander-in-chief. Disguised as a chauffeur, laborer, or gardener, he traveled throughout Africa and Europe, building up support for the ANC.

After his capture in 1962, Mandela was sentenced to five years in prison. But he was brought to court again soon afterward and charged with plotting to overthrow the government. Mandela and seven other ANC leaders, including Walter Sisulu, entered the high-security Robben Island Prison to serve life sentences.

On trial in 1963, Mandela wore traditional Xhosa dress and declared, "I have cherished the ideal of a democratic and free society in which all persons live together in harmony and with equal opportunities."

Prisoners were segregated by race on Robben Island, with black prisoners receiving fewer privileges and rations. During the day Mandela was put to work mining slate, sewing clothes, or repairing mail bags in the fierce sun. At night he was locked into a tiny cell. He had no newspapers, radio, or television and was allowed to write and receive just one letter every six months and see one visitor each year for a mere 30 minutes.

Life for prisoner 466/64 was incredibly difficult, but Mandela refused to give up hope, even after his mother and eldest son died. He was not allowed to attend either funeral.

Members of the ANC's military wing flee after sabotaging power lines. The group was formed in 1961 and named *Umkhonto we Sizwe*, meaning "spear of the nation." It was commanded by Mandela.

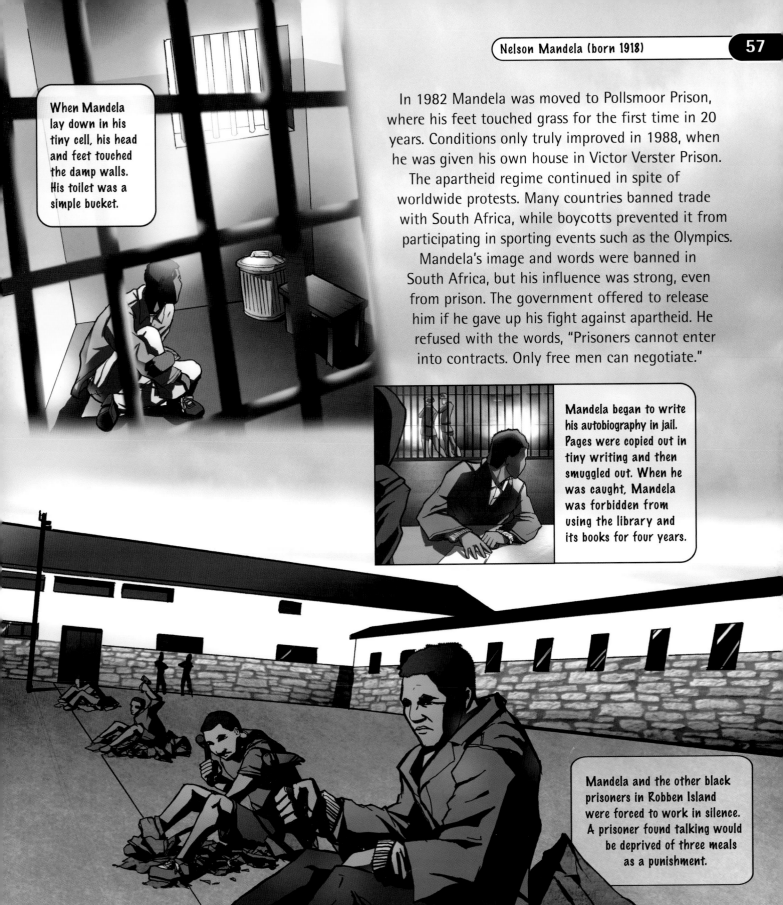

When Mandela lay down in his tiny cell, his head and feet touched the damp walls. His toilet was a simple bucket.

In 1982 Mandela was moved to Pollsmoor Prison, where his feet touched grass for the first time in 20 years. Conditions only truly improved in 1988, when he was given his own house in Victor Verster Prison. The apartheid regime continued in spite of worldwide protests. Many countries banned trade with South Africa, while boycotts prevented it from participating in sporting events such as the Olympics. Mandela's image and words were banned in South Africa, but his influence was strong, even from prison. The government offered to release him if he gave up his fight against apartheid. He refused with the words, "Prisoners cannot enter into contracts. Only free men can negotiate."

Mandela began to write his autobiography in jail. Pages were copied out in tiny writing and then smuggled out. When he was caught, Mandela was forbidden from using the library and its books for four years.

Mandela and the other black prisoners in Robben Island were forced to work in silence. A prisoner found talking would be deprived of three meals as a punishment.

On his release, Mandela and his wife Winnie, whom he married in 1958, were swamped by joyful supporters.

After 27 years in prison, it would have been easy for Mandela to use his new power for revenge. Instead, he dreamed of a South Africa where blacks and whites live side by side in peace. His government included black, Indian, and white South Africans—and even former supporters of apartheid. He set up the Truth and Reconciliation Commission, led by Archbishop Desmond Tutu, to investigate crimes of the past fairly and honestly.

Many black South Africans hated rugby, which was seen as a white sport. That changed when South Africa, supported by Mandela, won the rugby union World Cup in 1995.

In 1989 the ban on the ANC was lifted by South Africa's new president, Frederik Willem de Klerk. Nelson Mandela was released in February 1990, aged 71, amid scenes of great celebration. Soon he was made the president of the ANC and began to negotiate with the government to end apartheid.

Mandela and de Klerk jointly won the Nobel Peace Prize in December 1993, but a far more important event took place five months later. For the first time in South Africa's history, a democratic election was held in which all adults, regardless of race, were able to vote. The ANC won 252 of the 400 seats in the national assembly, and Nelson Mandela became South Africa's first black president.

Mandela hugs one of his guards as he leaves prison. Expecting a fiery terrorist out for revenge, many people were surprised by the intelligent and gentle man they encountered.

In 1999 Mandela stepped down as president. Instead of retiring quietly, he started campaigns to improve education for the world's poor and to battle AIDS. This disease has devastated Africa, killing more than 20 million people and leaving millions more very sick or orphaned. In 2005 Mandela's son Makgatho died from the disease.

His presidency was not perfect. He ordered the invasion of Lesotho and made alliances with controversial leaders such as Libya's Colonel Muammar Qaddafi. Mandela even admitted that his government could have done more to combat AIDS and poverty. Yet his dedication to creating a united South Africa and his willingness to forgive the people who kept him in prison have made him a hero to millions.

Mandela shows U.S. president Bill Clinton his old cell in Robben Island. He has spent a lot of time restoring South Africa's place in the world, helping reestablish sporting and cultural links with other countries.

Deep into retirement, Mandela still campaigns for charities and schools. In 2007 he became part of a group of dignitaries alongside Kofi Annan, the former head of the United Nations, whose aim is to "inspire hope where there is despair."

Other famous leaders

Benito Mussolini (1883–1945)

Italy's Benito Mussolini swept to power in 1922 as the leader of the right-wing Fascist Party, promising a return to the glories of the ancient Roman civilization. He boasted that Italy had won a new empire when it invaded Libya, Ethiopia, Eritrea, and Albania in the 1930s. During World War II, Mussolini formed an alliance with Adolf Hitler. The Italian armies were quickly repelled, however, and German forces had to rescue him in 1943. Two years later, he was captured and executed by Italian resistance fighters.

John F. Kennedy (1917–1963)

Intelligent and charismatic, John Fitzgerald Kennedy became the U.S.'s youngest president in 1960. He ordered the Bay of Pigs invasion of Cuba (see page 51) and sent military advisers to support South Vietnam in its war against communist North Vietnam. Kennedy and Soviet leader Nikita Khrushchev came to the brink of nuclear war during the 1962 Cuban Missile Crisis. One year later, Kennedy was shot dead while riding in a limousine through Dallas, Texas, an event that sent shock waves around the world.

ANC

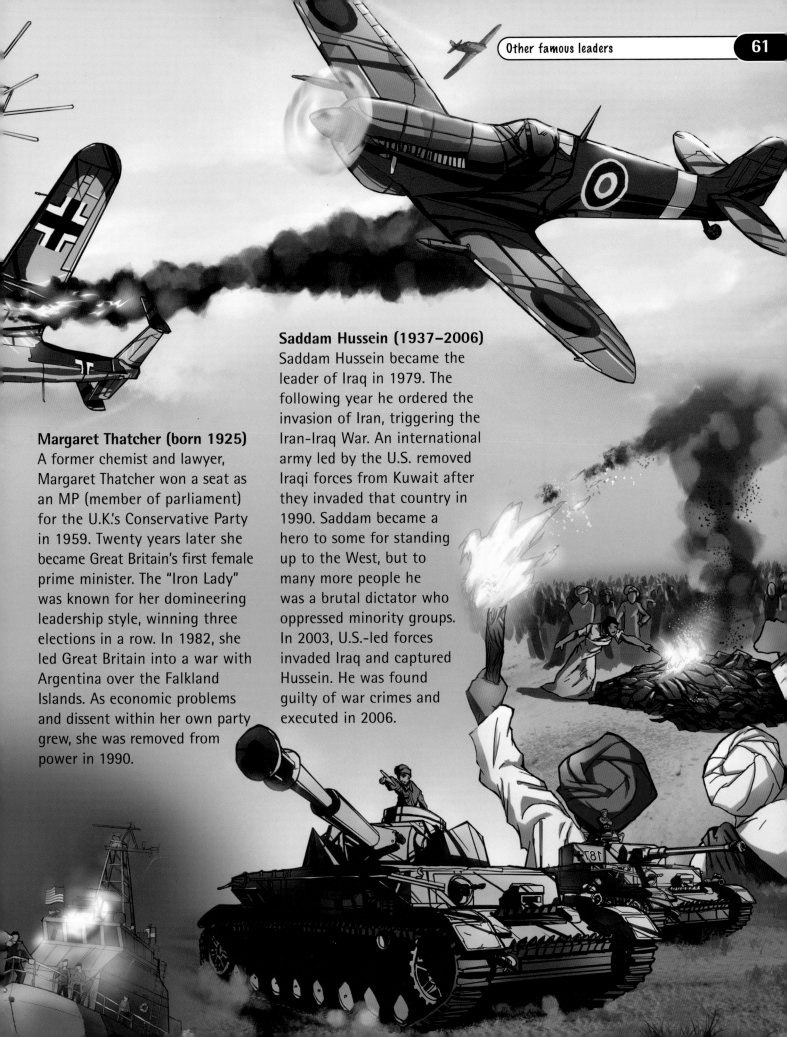

Margaret Thatcher (born 1925)
A former chemist and lawyer, Margaret Thatcher won a seat as an MP (member of parliament) for the U.K.'s Conservative Party in 1959. Twenty years later she became Great Britain's first female prime minister. The "Iron Lady" was known for her domineering leadership style, winning three elections in a row. In 1982, she led Great Britain into a war with Argentina over the Falkland Islands. As economic problems and dissent within her own party grew, she was removed from power in 1990.

Saddam Hussein (1937–2006)
Saddam Hussein became the leader of Iraq in 1979. The following year he ordered the invasion of Iran, triggering the Iran-Iraq War. An international army led by the U.S. removed Iraqi forces from Kuwait after they invaded that country in 1990. Saddam became a hero to some for standing up to the West, but to many more people he was a brutal dictator who oppressed minority groups. In 2003, U.S.-led forces invaded Iraq and captured Hussein. He was found guilty of war crimes and executed in 2006.

Glossary

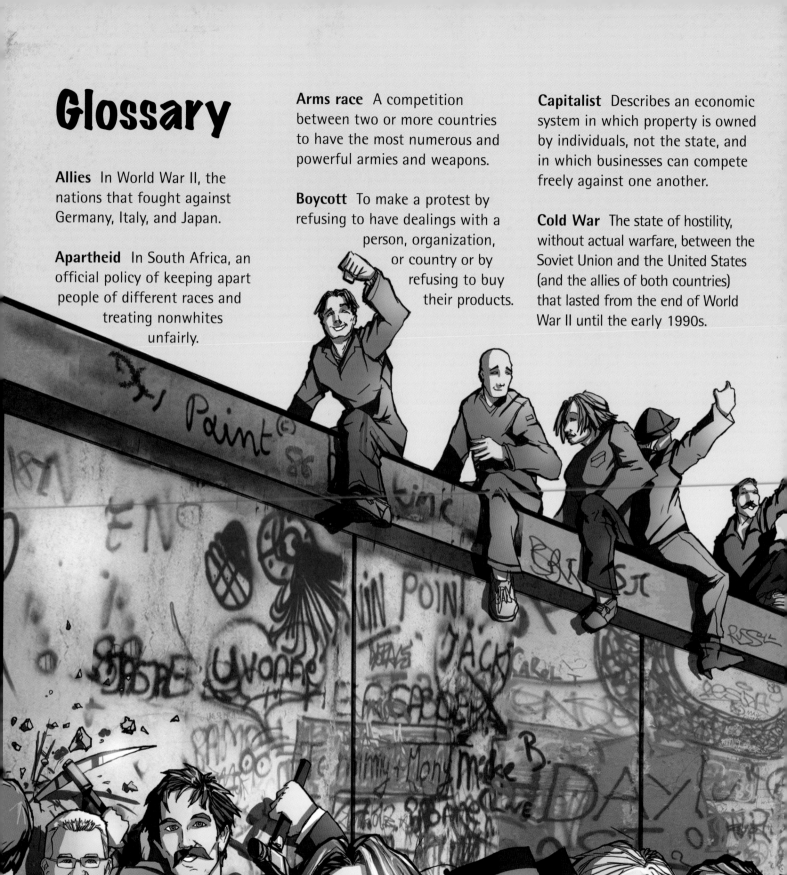

Allies In World War II, the nations that fought against Germany, Italy, and Japan.

Apartheid In South Africa, an official policy of keeping apart people of different races and treating nonwhites unfairly.

Arms race A competition between two or more countries to have the most numerous and powerful armies and weapons.

Boycott To make a protest by refusing to have dealings with a person, organization, or country or by refusing to buy their products.

Capitalist Describes an economic system in which property is owned by individuals, not the state, and in which businesses can compete freely against one another.

Cold War The state of hostility, without actual warfare, between the Soviet Union and the United States (and the allies of both countries) that lasted from the end of World War II until the early 1990s.

Colony A settlement or territory set up by a group of people from a distant country that is ruled by that country.

Communism A system of government based, in theory, on the state controlling the economy and in which wealth and goods are shared equally by the people.

Communist Describes a political and economic system based, in theory, on workers owning what they produce.

Concentration camp A guarded prison camp in which nonmilitary prisoners are held.

Coup A sudden attempt to overthrow a government, often by force.

Democratic Describes a system of government in which the people of a country elect their own leaders.

Dictator A leader who has total control over a country, usually unelected and ruling by force.

Genocide A policy of deliberately killing an entire race of people.

Guerrilla warfare A type of warfare in which small groups of fighters make surprise attacks.

Liberation The setting free of a country from foreign occupation.

Persecuted Treated unfairly, often because of political or religious beliefs.

Reform Making something better by changing it.

Regime A particular government or system of government.

Resistance In a war, an illegal organization that fights to set free a country that has been invaded by another country.

Show trial A highly public, unfair trial in which the accused does not have the chance to defend him or herself properly.

Soviet Union A communist country that existed from 1922 to 1991, made up of Russia and 14 other republics.

Superpower An extremely powerful country.

Township In South Africa under apartheid, a settlement specially created for nonwhite people to live in, often with few facilities.

Welfare system A system in which the government takes care of its citizens' social welfare—their health, education, housing, etc.

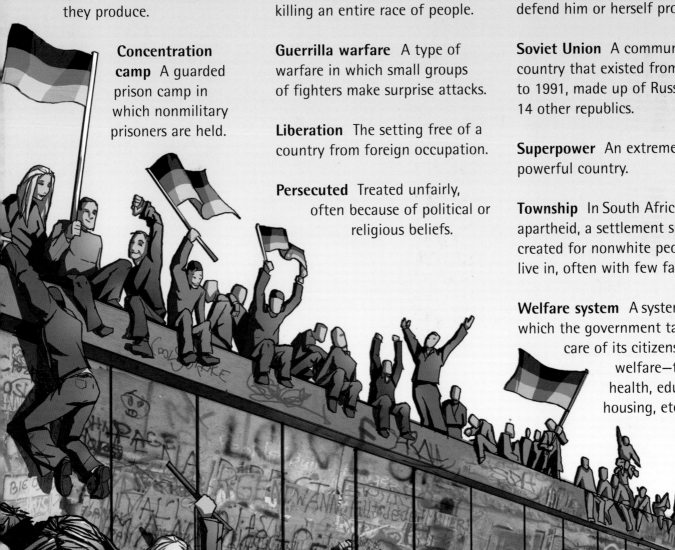
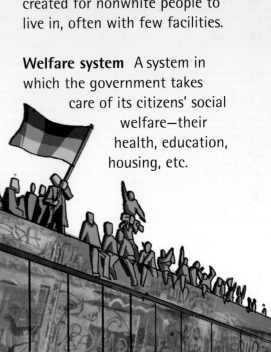

Index